Michelangelo

Andrew Langley

Published by Raintree, a division of Reed Elsevier, Inc.

Project Editors: Marta Segal Block, Helena Attlee
Production Manager: Brian Suderski
Designed by Ian Winton

Planned and produced by Discovery Books

Library of Congress Cataloging-in-Publication Data:

Langley, Andrew.
Michelangelo / Andrew Langley.
v. cm. -- (Raintree biographies)
Includes bibliographical references and index.
Contents: The wonderful statue -- Motherless child -- In the workshop --
The Medici family -- Early travels -- Rivals -- Orders from the Pope --
On the ceiling -- Farewell to Florence -- The Last Judgment -- Architect
and poet -- The final years -- The legacy of Michelangelo.
ISBN 0-7398-6864-0 (HC), 1-4109-0070-3 (Pbk.)
1. Michelangelo Buonarroti, 1475-1564--Juvenile literature. 2.
Artists--Italy--Biography--Juvenile literature. [1. Michelangelo
Buonarroti, 1475-1564. 2. Artists.] I. Title. II. Series.
N6923.B9L32 2003
709'.2--dc21

2002155031

Printed and bound in the United States
1 2 3 4 5 6 7 8 9 0 08 07 06 05 04 03

Acknowledgments
The publishers would like to thank the following for permission to reproduce their pictures:
The Bridgeman Art Library, pages cover, 4,6,7,8,9,10,11,13, 16, 17, 18, 20, 21, 22, 27;
Corbis, 5 (top), 12, 14, 19, 23, 25, 26, 28, 29; Mary Evans Picture Library, 5 (bottom);
Peter Newark's Pictures, 15, 24.

Some words are shown in bold, **like this**.
You can find out what they mean by looking in the glossary.

CONTENTS

THE WONDERFUL STATUE

One day in 1504, men brought a huge statue into the main square of Florence, Italy. There was a lot of excitement. Florence was home to many great artists, but this was special—it was the latest work from Michelangelo, the city's greatest artist.

The statue, which stood over 12 feet (4 meters) high, was of the **biblical** figure David. City leaders came to inspect the work. One called out that the nose was too thick. Annoyed, Michelangelo decided to play a trick. He secretly grabbed some **marble** dust and then pretended to chip away at the nose, letting the dust trickle through his fingers. This fooled the official, who said, "Ah, that's much better." In fact, the nose was just the same!

Carved from a huge, single block of marble, Michelangelo's David *is one of the most famous statues in the world.*

A Living Legend

"Anyone who has seen Michelangelo's David *has no need to see anything else by any other* **sculptor***, living or dead."*

Giorgio Vasari, *Lives of the Artists.*

Giant Killer

In the Bible story, David was a boy who saved his country by killing the giant Goliath. Michelangelo chose to show him as a strong warrior, staring boldly ahead. His statue represented the proud spirit of the city of Florence, defying its enemies.

People agreed that Michelangelo's **sculpture** of David was a masterpiece. But the artist went on to prove that he was also a dazzling painter, as well as an **architect**, designer, and poet.

Over 400 years have passed since Michelangelo's death, but many people still consider him the greatest artist that ever lived.

MOTHERLESS CHILD

Michelangelo Buonarroti was born on March 6, 1475, at Caprese in the province of Tuscany, Italy. His father was mayor of the village, but this job soon ended and the family returned to their hometown of Florence.

An unknown artist painted this view of Florence in 1490. It shows all the buildings that would have been there when Michelangelo, then aged 15, was living in the city.

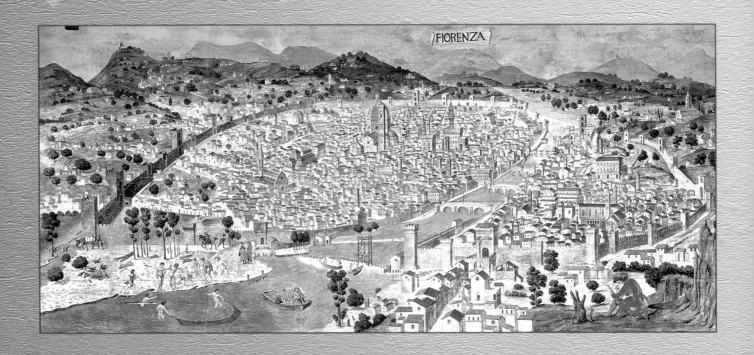

THE RENAISSANCE

At this time Florence was at the center of an astonishing explosion of enthusiasm for **scholarship** as well as all kinds of art. We call this period the Renaissance. Many great Italian painters, **sculptors**, writers, and **scholars** made Florence their home. Together they developed new techniques and a new way of seeing the world.

This picture, The School of Athens, *was painted by Raphael. Like Michelangelo, Raphael was Italian, too, and also one of the greatest artists of the Renaissance.*

Michelangelo was the second of five sons. His mother was too weak to feed him as a baby, so he was nursed by the wife of a local stonecutter. In later life, he once joked that her milk had given him his love of stone, hammers, and **chisels**.

Michelangelo's mother died when he was only six years old. At school he soon showed a very special talent for drawing. His father wanted him to become a banker or businessman, but Michelangelo was determined to be an artist. Despite punishments, he finally got his way. In 1488, he entered the workshop of a local artist to learn the art of painting.

IN THE WORKSHOP

In those days people saw artists as craftspeople who made products, just like carpenters or shoemakers. They would spend years learning the skills of their trade in a workshop, then set out to earn their living.

*This marble **relief** carved by Nanni di Banco (1384-1421) shows artists and craftspeople at work.*

So Michelangelo began his **career** in the workshop of a well-known Florentine painter, Domenico Ghirlandaio. Here he was taught everything from grinding colors for paints to making gold jewelry. Perhaps the most valuable lessons of all were in **fresco** work—painting pictures on the wet plaster of walls and ceilings.

A Master and His Apprentices

A master painter like Ghirlandaio was often hired to paint large pictures in churches. He probably did not carry out all the work himself, but sketched the outlines and filled in the most important areas, such as the faces or hands. His apprentices did the rest.

Ghirlandaio quickly realized that his new **apprentice** had an amazing talent. Once, Michelangelo was helping with work in a chapel. In a spare moment he started sketching what he saw: the **scaffolding**, tools, and materials, as well as the young men using them. When Ghirlandaio saw the sketch, he said, "This boy knows more about it than I do!"

Ghirlandaio was the best fresco artist in Florence. This is a detail from a much larger fresco called The Life of St. Francis.

THE MEDICI FAMILY

The richest and most powerful people in Florence were the Medicis. The head of the family was Lorenzo, who used his wealth to make the city more beautiful by hiring the best artists and **architects** to work for him. No wonder he was known as Lorenzo the Magnificent.

*Shown in a **fresco** by Benozzo Gozzoli, Lorenzo the Magnificent is depicted as one of the Three Kings, on his way to see the baby Jesus.*

The Broken Nose

Not everyone liked Michelangelo. He sometimes made fun of students less talented than himself. One of them, named Pietro Torrigiano, finally lost his temper and punched Michelangelo in the face. The result was a broken nose, which can clearly be seen in **portraits** of the artist.

Lorenzo had a garden full of ancient **sculptures**. He asked Ghirlandaio to send along any of his pupils who were interested in sculpture, so that they could study and learn from his collection. Among the first was Michelangelo. He was thrilled by the great works of the past, and soon impressed Lorenzo with his natural skill at carving.

In 1490 Michelangelo left the workshop, at the age of only 15. He went to live in the Medici's household, where Lorenzo treated him like a son. Over the next months, he produced his first sculptures, including a beautiful panel called *Battle of the* **Centaurs**.

Michelangelo took the subject for his Battle of the Centaurs *from a Greek* **myth**. *It gave the young artist a chance to practice carving the human body.*

EARLY TRAVELS

Lorenzo de' Medici died suddenly in April 1492. This was the second tragedy of Michelangelo's young life, and it left him without an employer or **protector**. Generally it was a bad time, as Florence was in a state of unrest and the Medici family was becoming unpopular.

Michelangelo left Florence and went to Venice and Bologna in 1494. When he returned a year later, things had grown even

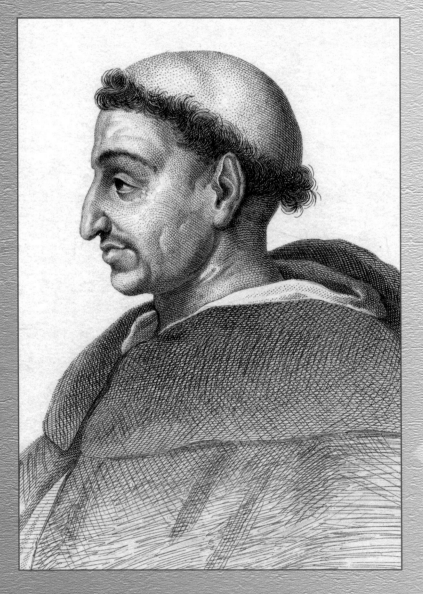

worse. Florence had fallen to the French, the Medici family had disappeared, and the city's ruler was a **fanatical** monk called Savonarola. Many were dying from **plague** or **famine**. It was perhaps not surprising that Michelangelo was soon on the road again.

Savonarola preached terrifying sermons, persuading the people of Florence to burn their fine clothes and jewels, and to give up their luxurious lifestyles.

This time he went to Rome, where he completed his first great work in 1499. It was the *Pietà*, a beautiful **marble** statue of the dead Jesus lying in the arms of his mother, Mary. Michelangelo's skill in carving details such as the hands and faces seemed almost miraculous. The **sculpture** made him famous.

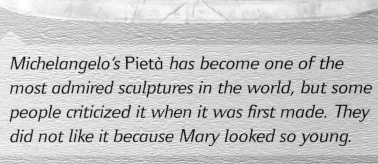

Michelangelo's Pietà *has become one of the most admired sculptures in the world, but some people criticized it when it was first made. They did not like it because Mary looked so young.*

Maker's Mark

Roman people flocked to see the *Pietà*, but no one knew who had carved it. One day, Michelangelo was surprised and irritated to hear someone say that the statue was made by a Milanese artist called Gobbo. That night he carved his own name very clearly on Mary's sash. It was the only work he ever signed.

RIVALS

After five years, Michelangelo returned to Florence. It was now 1501, and the city was calm again. Savonarola had been put to death and the French soldiers had gone. Michelangelo was welcomed by the new governor, and given a huge block of **marble** to carve. The result was his wonderful statue of David.

Michelangelo painted this picture of the Madonna around 1504. It shows the baby Jesus with Mary and Joseph.

Another, even more famous Florentine artist had also come home—his name was Leonardo da Vinci. Michelangelo and Leonardo did not like each other. Even so, in 1504 they found themselves working in the same building. Each was hired to paint a big battle scene on the walls of the city's council hall.

The two rivals set to work in competition. They drew up plans and made sketches for their two grand pictures. Sadly, the project was never finished, because both artists were called away to other work. For Michelangelo this meant a journey back to Rome.

Leonardo Da Vinci

Born near Florence in 1452, Leonardo created some of the best-known paintings in the world, including the *Last Supper* and the *Mona Lisa*. Yet he was also a scientist and designer (of everything from cannons to flying machines) and a **pioneer** in the study of the human body.

Leonardo da Vinci's famous Mona Lisa *was a picture of the wife of a Florentine official.*

ORDERS FROM THE POPE

There was a new Pope in Rome named Julius II. He was determined to make the city a grander and more beautiful place. In 1505 he ordered Michelangelo to come to Rome and design a huge **tomb** for him.

This was a great honor for Michelangelo. He immediately started on the work, and hurried off to the **marble quarries** in the mountains of Carrara. It was important to choose exactly the right blocks of stone for the job.

Pope Julius II, painted here by Raphael, employed Michelangelo to work in Rome.

Michelangelo stayed in Carrara for eight months. The longer he stayed, the bigger and more expensive his tomb designs grew. Eventually, Pope Julius II lost his patience and refused to pay any more. He even refused to speak to Michelangelo. The **sculptor** returned angrily to Florence.

Marble Mountains

Carrara, near Florence, is still famous today for its marble. Michelangelo wandered through the mountains with two helpers, selecting the stones he wanted. Workers then transported the blocks down to the coast and put them on barges, which took them to Rome by sea.

*This **fresco** was painted in about 1465 by Andrea Mantegna. It shows men at work in a marble quarry near Rome.*

The Pope tried several times to call Michelangelo back, but the sculptor refused to return. It was not until late in 1506 that the pair met again. Now Julius had a brand-new project for him— to paint a whole ceiling!

ON THE CEILING

In the center of Rome stands the Vatican, the palace where the Pope, the head of the Catholic Church, lives. And at the center of the Vatican is the Sistine Chapel. The chapel ceiling had been painted to look like the night sky, but Julius II wanted something more startling. He hired Michelangelo to repaint the ceiling.

Michelangelo tried to get out of the job, saying that he was a **sculptor** and not a painter. The Pope insisted, and in 1508 Michelangelo began work. It was a mammoth task for one man, because the ceiling was huge. Worse still, the artist had to stand on a tall **scaffolding** and bend backwards so that he could paint above his head.

Michelangelo painted Jonah at one end of the ceiling. He is about to be swallowed by the whale to the right.

This picture of God, in the act of creating Adam, forms one of the four central panels of the ceiling.

Somehow, Michelangelo managed to cope with an aching back and paint dripping on his face. He painted the Bible story of God creating the world. He showed other Bible stories, ending with Noah and the Flood.

Painting a Fresco

Fresco is the Italian word for fresh. A fresco picture is painted with water-based colors on the fresh, or still-wet, plaster of a wall or ceiling. The artist has to work quickly before the plaster dries, and accurately, because mistakes are hard to correct. The Sistine Chapel ceiling is a fresco.

FAREWELL TO FLORENCE

In 1512 the Sistine Chapel ceiling was **unveiled** at last. "It was such as to make everyone speechless with astonishment," reported one writer. Michelangelo's fame was now even greater, but he was about to enter a long and unhappy period.

For a start, Pope Julius II died and work began again on his **tomb**. Once more, Michelangelo was unable to finish it, and by 1517 he was back in Florence. Here he started a series of major projects for his old employers, the Medici family.

This magnificent reading room is in the Laurentian Library that Michelangelo designed for the Medici family in Florence.

Absent-minded Genius

When he was hard at work, Michelangelo forgot about everything else. He ate and slept little, and would hardly ever change his clothes. Sometimes he left his pants on so long that they stuck to his legs!

Michelangelo also turned in another new direction: toward **architecture**. He was hired to design a chapel for the Medici family, as well as a library nearby, but luck appeared to be against him. He never completed the chapel, because the Medici family was driven out of Florence again. The new city leaders hired Michelangelo to plan new **fortifications**. Then, the Medicis returned and accused Michelangelo of being a **traitor**.

This is a sketch, or design, for the Medici Chapel by Michelangelo.

Michelangelo decided that he must leave Florence for ever. The perfect opportunity arrived in 1534 when he was called back to Rome—and to the Sistine Chapel.

THE LAST JUDGMENT

When Michelangelo settled in Rome, he hoped that he could at last finish Julius's **tomb**. But the new Pope, Paul III, had other ideas. He appointed Michelangelo as his chief **architect**, **sculptor**, and painter, and ordered him to concentrate on one single work—another **fresco** for the Sistine Chapel.

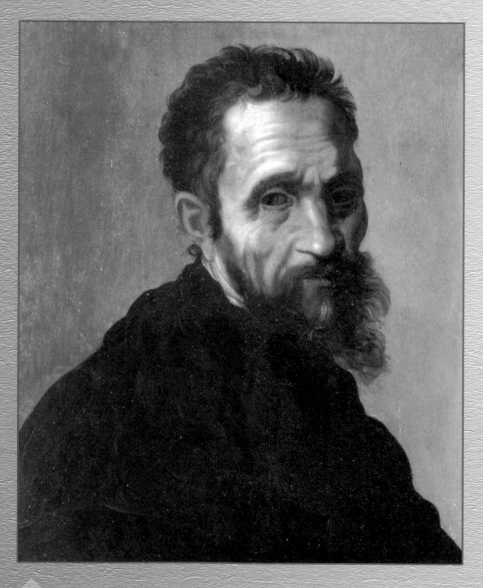

*Jacopo del Conte's **portrait** of Michelangelo shows the artist as an elderly man.*

This fresco would be painted on the wall above the altar, and would complete the Bible story by showing the Judgment Day. It was another massive challenge. Michelangelo labored over for more than seven years, once falling from the **scaffolding** and injuring his leg.

The Last Judgment is a much grimmer and darker work than the ceiling **fresco**. Its crowded figures are full of horror and despair. Michelangelo was able to convey the "terribleness" of this story in a way that no other artist had ever been able to do.

Michelangelo Writes About Sculpture

Even the best artist never has an idea
*Which a **marble** block does not contain*
Already within its shell, and he'll only reach it
If his hand obeys his brain.

This detail from Michelangelo's Last Judgment *shows the arrival of the **damned** in hell.*

ARCHITECT AND POET

Michelangelo reached his 70th birthday in 1545. During the rest of his life he did little more painting, but he still worked with blazing energy as an **architect**, trying to finish the many projects that he had started.

His most urgent project was the **tomb** of Julius II, which had first been **commissioned** 40 years earlier! The monument was smaller than he had planned, but at last it was complete. Next, Michelangelo designed a palace and a grand public square for the center of Rome, called the Campidoglio. In 1547 he became the official architect for the church of St. Peter's in Rome.

An engraving of St. Peter's in Rome, made in the 16th century.

Michelangelo drew detailed plans for the Campidoglio, but very little of the square was built before he died.

Michelangelo the Poet

Michelangelo was a poet as well as an artist. Some of his finest poems were inspired by the two most important relationships in his life. He had great friendships with the handsome Tommaso de' Cavalieri, and a noblewoman named Vittoria Colonna. His verses record his feelings for his friends, and his strong belief in God. But many also show that he was ill, and knew that death was not far away.

THE FINAL YEARS

After a lifetime of hard work, Michelangelo was stooped and unable to raise his head. Even so, he could hammer chips out of hard **marble** more quickly than younger men. He carved at night, wearing a paper hat with a candle on top to light his work. In 1555 he began a major **sculpture**, another *Pietà*. But he soon grew unhappy with it and attacked the piece with his hammer, breaking off arms and legs.

Michelangelo's last great work was to plan the **dome** on top of St. Peter's church. In 1561 he made a wooden model of the dome, but the building was not actually finished until long after his death.

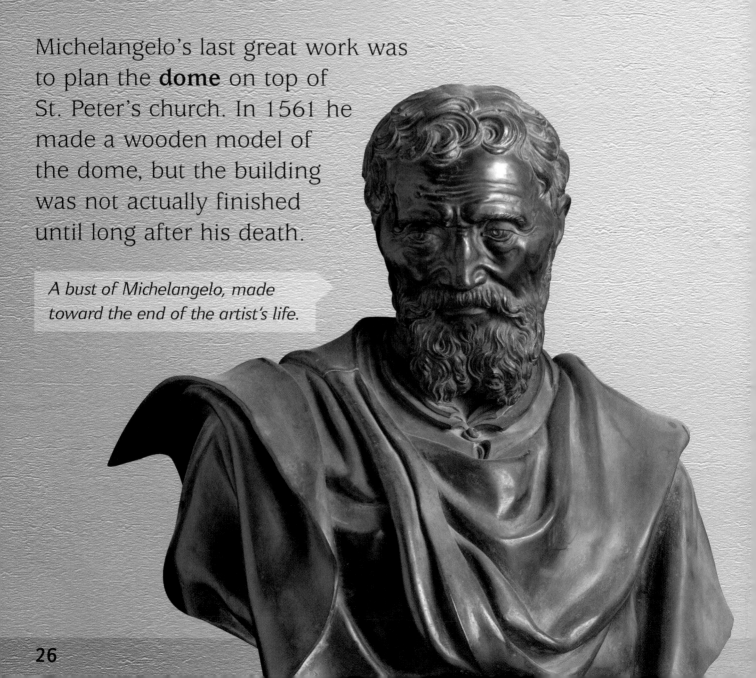

A bust of Michelangelo, made toward the end of the artist's life.

A Leading Light

Michelangelo was once asked what he thought about a **sculptor** who copied **antique** statues. He replied, *"No one who follows others can ever get in front of them, and those who can't do good work on their own can hardly make use of what others have done."*

Michelangelo died at the age of 88 in February 1564. He was buried in Rome, but soon after this his body was secretly taken back to Florence. It lies there today in the church of Santa Croce, beneath a marble **tomb**.

Giorgio Vasari designed a tomb for Michelangelo, the man he regarded as the greatest sculptor the world had ever seen.

The Legacy of Michelangelo

During his lifetime, Michelangelo was seen as a genius whose **sculpture** was as good as anything made by the Ancient Greeks or Romans. He had a huge influence on the **sculptors**, painters, and **architects** of his time.

Time has left its mark on many of Michelangelo's works. The statue of David, for example, had to be moved indoors because it was being damaged by the weather. A copy now stands in its place. His famous *Pietà* has needed careful **restoration**.

The damaged face of the Virgin, before the restoration of Michelangelo's Pietà.

FRAGILE FRESCOES

The survival of the Sistine ceiling is surprising. Cracks appeared in the **fresco** in 1547, and had to be quickly filled in. The painting was cleaned in 1625 and 1710, when someone covered it in clear glue. In 1797 part of the ceiling fell in. In 1980 complete restoration began, to clean off the centuries of dust, grease, and soot, as well as the glue.

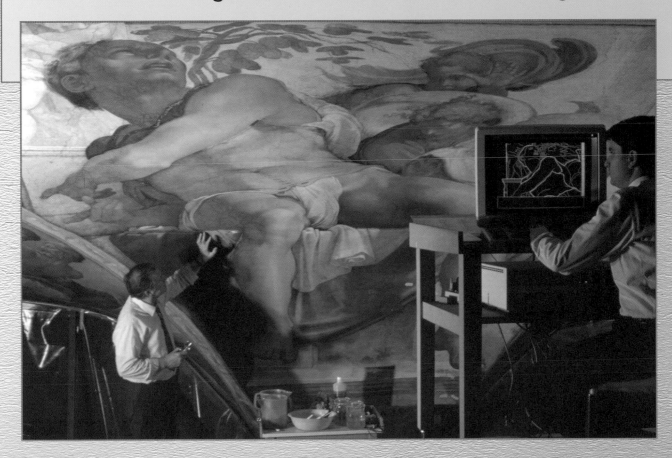

Computer technology was used during the restoration of the frescoes on the ceiling of the Sistine Chapel.

Today the masterpieces of Michelangelo are known all over the world. Most are still in Italy, where they attract millions of visitors every year. Images of his work can be found everywhere, from the **dome** of the U.S. Capitol building to the tiny models of David sold in souvenir shops.

TIMELINE

1475 - March 6 – Michelangelo Buonarroti born in Caprese, Tuscany

1481 – Michelangelo's mother dies

1488 – Becomes an apprentice in Ghirlandaio's workshop in Florence

1490 – Joins the household of Lorenzo de' Medici; carves earliest sculptures

1492 – Death of Lorenzo

1494 – Travels to Venice and Bologna

1497 – Travels to Rome

1499 – Completes the *Pietà*

1501 – Returns to Florence

1501-1504 – At work on the statue of David

1504 – Starts design for battle painting, in competition with Leonardo

1505 – To Rome again, receives first contract to design tomb for Pope Julius II

1506 – Home to Florence; signs contract for Sistine Chapel ceiling

1512 – Completes the ceiling of Sistine Chapel

1520 – Begins work on the Medici Chapel in Florence

1529 – Designs fortifications to defend Florence

1532 – Meets Tommaso de' Cavalieri

1534 – Begins work on *The Last Judgment* in Sistine Chapel

1536 – Meets Vittoria Colonna

1541 – Completes *The Last Judgment*

1542 – Receives fifth and final contract for Julius's tomb

1546 – Designs new city square for Rome (the Campidoglio)

1547 – Appointed as official architect of new St. Peter's; death of Vittoria Colonna

1555 – Begins work on the Florence *Pietà* (later damaged)

1558 – Begins designs for the St. Peter's dome

1564 – Death of Michelangelo

GLOSSARY

antique something made at an earlier or ancient time

apprentice someone who signs an agreement to learn a trade or craft from a master

architect person who designs buildings

architecture process of designing buildings

biblical to do with the Bible

career progress through life, especially in work

centaur imaginary horse with human arms and head

chisel metal tool with a sharp edge used for cutting stone or wood

commission to instruct someone to do a job, such as painting a picture of making a sculpture

contract formal agreement to do something

damned people in hell

dome rounded roof on top of a building

famine very bad shortage of food

fanatic person who is very enthusiastic, or too enthusiastic, about something

fortification the building of walls and towers to strengthen a place against attack

fresco painting done on damp plaster

legacy something left by a previous generation

marble special kind of limestone that is polished and used in sculpture or building

myth old story about ancient times

pietà painting or sculpture of the Virgin Mary holding the body of Jesus (from the Italian for "pity")

pioneer one of first people to go to a place or investigate a new subject

plague dangerous illness that spreads very quickly

portrait picture of a person

protector person who keeps someone safe from harm or injury

quarry place where stone or other mineral is extracted

relief method of making a picture or pattern that stands out from the surface

restoration putting something back in its original condition

scaffolding framework of wood or metal holding up a raised platform or work surface

scholar person who has studied a subject very thoroughly

scholarship scholar's knowledge

sculptor person who makes sculptures

sculpture shape carved from wood, stone or metal

tomb vault or chamber where a dead body is placed

traitor someone who betrays his country or community

unveil reveal

FURTHER READING

Lacey, Sue, and Antony Mason. *In the Time of Michelangelo: The Renaissance Period.* Brookfield, Ct: Millbrook Press, 2001.

Stanley, Diane. *Michelangelo*, New York, HarperCollins, 2000.

Venezia, Mike. *Getting to Know the World's Greatest Artists: Michelangelo.* New York, Scholastic Library, 1991.

Woodhouse, Jane. and Richard Tames. *The Life and Work of Michelangelo Buonarroti.* Heinemann, 2001.

INDEX